Love Is Like the Lion's Tooth

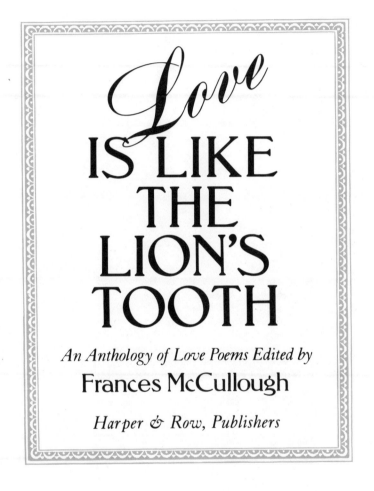

Love
IS LIKE
THE
LION'S
TOOTH

An Anthology of Love Poems Edited by
Frances McCullough

Harper & Row, Publishers

*Library of Congress Cataloging in Publication Data
Main entry under title:*

Love is like the lion's tooth.

  *Summary: A collection of poems about the various
stages and effects of love.*
  *1. Love poetry. 2. Children's poetry. [1. Love
poetry] I. McCullough, Frances Monson, 1938–*
PN6110.L6L48 1982   808.81'9354   77-25659
ISBN 0-06-024138-1   AACR2
ISBN 0-06-024139-X (lib. bdg.)

First Edition

Acknowledgments

Contents

A Note to the Reader   *xiv*

Strawberries   *Edwin Morgan*   *1*

Song   *Ted Hughes*   *2*

You Have What I Look For   *Jaime Sabines*   *3*

Song   *Azande, from the Congo (Zaire)*   *3*

Charm   *Miklos Radnoti*   *4*

✳ Waiting   *Yevgeny Yevtushenko*   *5.*

Love   *Lady Izumi*   *5*

His Legs Ran About   *Ted Hughes*   *6*

Untitled   *Petronius Arbiter*   *7*

Hesitating Ode   *Miklos Radnoti*   *8*

A Spring Song of Tzu-Yeh   *Hsiao Yen*   *9*

Brown Penny   *William Butler Yeats*   *9*

White World   *H.D.*   *10*

✳ I Hid You   *Miklos Radnoti*   *11*

Unknown Love   *Lady Otomo of Sakanone*   *12*

#15 from Nineteen Pieces for Love   *Susan Griffin*   *12*

Valentine   *Donald Hall*   *13*

Untitled   *E. E. Cummings*   *14*

Untitled   *Bhavabhūti*   *15*

Untitled   *E. E. Cummings*   *16*

What There Is   *Kenneth Patchen*   *17*

Names of Horses   *Donald Hall*   *18*

Poem in Which My Legs Are Accepted   *Kathleen Fraser*   *20*

I'd Want Her Eyes to Fill With Wonder   *Kenneth Patchen*   *22*

Love Comes Quietly   *Robert Creeley*   *23*

Sleeping With Someone Who Came in Secret   *Lady Ise*   *23*

Untitled   *Yvonne Caroutch*   *24*

At Mid-Ocean   *Robert Bly*   *24*

from The Princess   *Alfred, Lord Tennyson*   *25*

from Razón de Amor   *Pedro Salinas*   *26*

I Am He That Aches With Love   *Walt Whitman*   *27*

from The Song of Solomon, Chapter 2   *28*

He Remembers Forgotten Beauty   *William Butler Yeats*   *29*

The Dream   *Theodore Roethke*   *30*

Lullaby   *W. H. Auden*   *32*

Poem   *Frank O'Hara*   *34*

Song   *Ruth Krauss*   *35*

Inanna's Song   *Ancient Sumerian*   *35*

Song   *W. D. Snodgrass*   *36*

Simple-Song   *Marge Piercy*   *37*

The Hardness Scale   *Joyce Peseroff*   *38*

Perversity   *Susan Griffin*   *40*

Song   *Sanskrit*   *41*

Betrothed   *Louise Bogan*   *42*

People   *Orhan Veli Kanik*   *43*

Untitled   *Anonymous, Early English*   *43*

On Love   *Kyōgoku Tamekane*   *44*

Mirage   *Christina Rossetti*   *45*

Being Sad   *Orhan Veli Kanik*   *45* from The Walls Do Not Fall   *H. D.*   *46*

Lock the Place in Your Heart   *Zindzi Mandela*   *47*

Heart! We Will Forget Him   *Emily Dickinson*   *47*

Untitled   *Maureen Owen*   *48*

The Alchemist   *Louise Bogan*   *49*

The Winter Moon   *Tagaki Kyozo*   *50*

from 9 Verses of the Same Song   *Wendell Berry*   *51*

Swahili Love Song   *Anonymous*   *52*

Insomnia   *Elizabeth Bishop*   *53*

Girl's Song   *Tuareg, from the Sahara*   *54*

End Song   *Ruth Krauss*   *55*

Untitled   *Natalya Gorbanyevskaya*   *55*

A Painful Love Song   *Yehuda Amichai*   *56*

Untitled   *Edna St. Vincent Millay*   *57*

Epilogue   *Denise Levertov*   *58*

Seizure   *Sappho*   *59*

Colors   *Yevgeny Yevtushenko*   *60*

Untitled   *Sister Bertke, Hermitess of Utrecht*   *61*

Ghazal XII   *Mirza Ghalib*   *62*

The Fist   *Derek Walcott*   *63*

To Carry On Living   *Yehuda Amichai*   *64*

The Radiance   *Kabir*   *65*

Movement   *Denise Levertov*   *66*

A Blessing   *James Wright*   *67*

Untitled   *Rumi*   *68*

Untitled   *Yunus Emre*   *70*

Things I Didn't Know I Loved   *Nazim Hikmet*   *71*

Index of Authors   *76*

Index of Titles   *77*

Index of First Lines   *79*

Love is not primarily a relationship to a specific person; it is an *attitude*, an *orientation of character* which determines the relatedness of a person to the world as a whole, not toward one "object" of love.

Erich Fromm
The Art of Loving

Lack-love, sing some sweetness into your bones.
Theodore Roethke

Love is like the lion's tooth.
William Butler Yeats

A Note to the Reader

In my own adolescence, which took place in the Fifties, I spent a considerable amount of time pursuing the secret of life—in libraries, in churches, in obscure philosophies, in art, in conjunction with certain extraordinary people in my vicinity. All too quickly sophistication crept in, and my friends—my fellow seekers—and I agreed with knowing smiles that life was, indeed, a river.

What I had no way of seeing then was that the secret itself had already happened to me, was coursing through me in waves of deep energy. No one seems to ask anymore, but for me one of the secrets is passion—that splendid combination of love, energy, and intensity that literally transforms the world. Children feel very deeply, but they are usually not passionate; they cannot go beyond the daily life on to new levels of conscious experience. It seems to me that passion is the special gift of adolescence, usually surfacing first in erotic feeling, but also in passions of the mind and the spirit, which are every bit as astonishing and satisfying as their bodily counterparts. So: these are love poems, yes, but they are really about passion.

Nothing, of course, beats falling in love and being loved back— as though you had been learning a strange new language by yourself and suddenly there is someone else who speaks it and you can't stop talking; someone who understands you deeply and releases a magical part of yourself of which you were not previously aware. In putting together this collection of poems, I've found a great number that speak of this exquisite experience. There have not been many from contemporary American women, and I don't entirely know why. The general pattern of the collection runs the typical love-course: from anticipation to intense feeling, then ecstasy, trouble, jealousy, bitterness, pain, reconciliation, and finally, on to a greater love of the world itself. Readers will note that I have taken a rather broad definition of love here—to include not only the opposite sex or the same sex, but also animals, the world of the spirit, and even that most elusive passion of all, the love that literally dares not speak its name: self-love.

The poems come from a great variety of times and places—not out of any desire to be diverse, but because that is where I found the particular quality I was after. I've resisted the temptation to use songs here, though certainly love has been the main subject of songs since the beginning of time. There are certain kinds of feelings—longing, for instance—to which music brings an extraordinary dimension that's forever missing on the page. This is especially true if you're in a real love agony.

But there's not much agony in this book. What I've tried to do here is look for those poems that speak directly to the reader's passionate self, so as to bring you as close to the fire as possible.

F.M.

STRAWBERRIES

There were never strawberries
like the ones we had
that sultry afternoon
sitting on the step
of the open french window
facing each other
your knees held in mine
the blue plates in our laps
the strawberries glistening
in the hot sunlight
we dipped them in sugar
looking at each other
not hurrying the feast
for one to come
the empty plates
laid on the stone together
with the two forks crossed
and I bent towards you
sweet in that air
in my arms
abandoned like a child
from your eager mouth
the taste of strawberries
in my memory
lean back again
let me love you
let the sun beat
on our forgetfulness
one hour of all
the heat intense
and summer lightning
on the Kilpatrick hills

let the storm wash the plates

Edwin Morgan

SONG

O lady, when the tipped cup of the moon blessed you
You became soft fire with a cloud's grace;
The difficult stars swam for eyes in your face;
You stood, and your shadow was my place:
You turned, your shadow turned to ice,
  O my lady.

O lady, when the sea caressed you
You were a marble of foam, but dumb.
When will the stone open its tomb?
When will the waves give over their foam?
You will not die, nor come home,
  O my lady.

O lady, when the wind kissed you
You made him music, for you were a shaped shell.
I follow the waters and the wind still
Since my heart heard it and all to pieces fell
Which your lovers stole, meaning ill,
  O my lady.

O lady, consider when I shall have lost you
The moon's full hands, scattering waste,
The sea's hands, dark from the world's breast,
The world's decay where the wind's hands have passed,
And my head, worn out with love, at rest
In my hands, and my hands full of dust,
  O my lady.

Ted Hughes

YOU HAVE WHAT I LOOK FOR

You have what I look for, what I long for, what I love,
you have it.
The fist of my heart is beating, calling.
I thank the stories for you,
I thank your mother and your father
and death who has not seen you.
I thank the air for you.
You are elegant as wheat,
delicate as the outline of your body.
I have never loved a slender woman
but you have made my hands fall in love,
you moored my desire,
you caught my eyes like two fish.
And for this I am at your door, waiting.

Jaime Sabines
Translated from the Spanish by W. S. Merwin

SONG

Desire for a woman took hold of me in the night
          oo like madness,
desire for a woman took hold of me in the night
          oo like madness.

Translated from the Azande, the Congo (Zaire)

CHARM

With trembling eyes
I sit in the light
a rosetree jumps
over the hedge
the light jumps too
clouds gather
lightning flashes
and already high up
wild thunder
answers
wild thunder
down below the blue
of lakes withers
the surfaces flood
come into the house
take off your dress
it's raining outside now
take off your shirt
let the rain wash
our hearts into one heart.

Miklos Radnoti

Translated from the Hungarian
by Steven Polgar, Stephen Berg
and S. J. Marks

WAITING

My love will come
will fling open her arms and fold me in them,
will understand my fears, observe my changes.
In from the pouring dark, from the pitch night
without stopping to bang the taxi door
she'll run upstairs through the decaying porch
burning with love and love's happiness,
she'll run dripping upstairs, she won't knock,
will take my head in her hands,
and when she drops her overcoat on a chair,
it will slide to the floor in a blue heap.

Yevgeny Yevtushenko
Translated from the Russian
by Robin Milner-Gulland and Peter Levi, S.J.

LOVE (from *Fifty-One Tanka*)

From Prince Atsumichi:
If I speak of love you'll think I am like everyone else, but my
heart

this morning is incomparable

Lady Izumi
Translated from the Japanese by Hiroaki Sato

HIS LEGS RAN ABOUT

Till they tangled and seemed to trip and lie down
With her legs intending to hold them there forever

His arms lifted things, groped in dark rooms, at last with their
                                                                hands
Caught her arms
And lay down enwoven at last at last

Mouth talked its way in and out and finally
Found her mouth and settled deeper deeper

His chest pushed until it came up against
Her breast at the end of everything

His navel fitted over her navel as closely as possible
Like a mirror face down flat on a mirror

And so when every part
Like a bull pushing towards its cows, not to be stayed
Like a calf seeking its mama
Like a desert staggerer, among his hallucinations
Seeking the hoof-churned hole

Finally got what it needed, and grew still, and closed its eyes

Then such greatness and truth descended

As over a new grave, when the mourners have gone
And the stars come out
And the earth, bristling and raw, tiny and lost,
Resumes its search

Rushing through the vast astonishment.

Ted Hughes

Doing, a filthy pleasure is, and short;
And done, we straight repent us of the sport:
Let us not then rush blindly on unto it,
Like lustful beasts, that only know to do it:
For lust will languish, and that heat decay.
But thus, thus, keeping endless holiday,
Let us together closely lie and kiss,
There is no labour, nor no shame in this;
This hath pleased, doth please, and long will please; never
Can this decay, but is beginning ever.

Petronius Arbiter
Translated from the Latin by Ben Jonson

HESITATING ODE

I've been planning to tell you
about the secret galaxy of my love for so long—
in just one image, just the essence.
But you are swarming and flooding inside me like
existence, as eternal and certain sometimes
as a snail shell changed to stone inside a stone.
Spattered by the moon, night curves over my head
and hunts for the little dreams that rustle
suddenly, then take flight. But I still can't
tell you what it really means to me when I write
and feel your warm glance above my hands.
Metaphors are useless. They come up. I drop them.
And tomorrow I'll begin the whole thing over again
because I'm worth about as much as the words
in this poem and because all this excites me until
I'm only bone and a few tufts of hair.
You are tired. I feel it too. It was a long day.
What else can I say? Objects look at each other
and praise you, half a cube of sugar sings
on the table, drops of honey fall and
glow on the tablecloth like beads of pure gold.
An empty glass clinks by itself,
happy because it lives with you. And maybe I'll
have time to tell you what it's like when it waits
for you to come back. Dreaming's slowly falling
darkness touches, touches me, flies off, then touches
your brow again. Your heavy lids say goodbye.
Your hair spreads out and flickers
and you sleep. The long shadow of your eyelashes
quivers. Your hand sinks on
my pillow, a birch branch going to sleep.
But I sleep in you also. You aren't "another" world.
And I can hear how the many mysterious,
thin, wise lines change
      in your cool palm.

         Miklos Radnoti

Translated from the Hungarian by Steven Polgar,
Stephen Berg and S. J. Marks

A SPRING SONG OF TZU-YEH

On the stairway fragrance assails the bosom;
In the garden flowers light the eye.
Once the spring heart is like this,
Love comes without bounds.

Hsiao Yen

Translated from the Chinese by Jan W. Walls

BROWN PENNY

I whispered, "I am too young."
And then, "I am old enough";
Wherefore I threw a penny
To find out if I might love.
"Go and love, go and love, young man,
If the lady be young and fair."
Ah, penny, brown penny, brown penny,
I am looped in the loops of her hair.

O love is the crooked thing,
There is nobody wise enough
To find out all that is in it,
For he would be thinking of love
Till the stars had run away
And the shadows eaten the moon.
Ah, penny, brown penny, brown penny,
One cannot begin it too soon.

William Butler Yeats

WHITE WORLD

The whole white world is ours,
and the world, purple with rose-bays,
bays, bush on bush,
group, thicket, hedge and tree,
dark islands in a sea
of grey-green olive or wild white-olive,
cut with the sudden cypress shafts,
in clusters, two or three,
or with the slender, single cypress-tree.

Slid from the hill,
as crumbling snow-peaks slide,
citron on citron fill
the valley, and delight
waits till our spirits tire
of forest, grove and bush
and purple flower of the laurel-tree.

Yet no one wearies,
joined is each to each
in happiness complete
with bush and flower:
ours is the wind-breath
at the hot noon-hour,
ours is the bee's soft belly,
and the blush of the rose-petal,
lifted, of the flower.

H.D.

I HID YOU

I hid you for a long time
the way a branch hides its
slowly ripening fruit among leaves,
and like a flower of sane ice
on a winter window
you open in my mind.
Now I know what it means
when your hand swoops up to your hair.
In my heart I keep
the small tilt of your ankle too
and I'm amazed by the delicate curve
of your ribs, coldly
like someone who has lived
such breathing miracles.
Still, in my dreams
I often have a hundred arms
and like god in a dream
I hold you in those arms.

Miklos Radnoti

*Translated from the Hungarian
by Steven Polgar, Stephen Berg
and S. J. Marks*

UNKNOWN LOVE

Unknown love
is bitter
as a virgin lily
on the summer
meadow,
blooming in bushes.

Lady Otomo of Sakanone
Translated from the Japanese
by Willis Barnstone

#15 from NINETEEN PIECES FOR LOVE

trying to say
suddenly
what I want
to possess
is not a woman
   not a man
but love
my own
  feeling

  Susan Griffin

VALENTINE

Chipmunks jump, and
Greensnakes slither.
Rather burst than
Not be with her.

Bluebirds fight, but
Bears are stronger.
We've got fifty
Years or longer.

Hoptoads hop, but
Hogs are fatter.
Nothing else but
Us can matter.

Donald Hall

i like my body when it is with your
body. It is so quite new a thing.
Muscles better and nerves more.
i like your body. i like what it does,
i like its hows. i like to feel the spine
of your body and its bones, and the trembling
-firm-smooth ness and which i will
again and again and again
kiss, i like kissing this and that of you,
i like, slowly stroking the, shocking fuzz
of your electric fur, and what-is-it comes
over parting flesh. . . . And eyes big love-crumbs,

and possibly i like the thrill

of under me you so quite new

E. E. Cummings

Deep in love
cheek leaning on cheek we talked
of whatever came to our minds
just as it came
slowly oh
slowly
with our arms twined
tightly around us
and the hours passed and we
did not know it
still talking when
the night had gone

Bhavabhūti, 8th century

Translated from the Sanskrit
by W. S. Merwin and J. Moussaieff Masson

your little voice
                    Over the wires came leaping
and I felt suddenly
dizzy
          With the jostling and shouting of merry flowers
wee skipping high-heeled flames
courtesied before my eyes
                              or twinkling over to my side
Looked up
with impertinently exquisite faces
floating hands were laid upon me
I was whirled and tossed into delicious dancing
up
UP
with the pale important
                    stars and the Humorous
                                        moon
dear girl
How i was crazy how i cried when i heard
                                        over time
and tide and death
leaping
Sweetly
          your voice

                                        E. E. Cummings

WHAT THERE IS

In this my green world
Flowers birds are hands
They hold me
I am loved all day
All this pleases me
I am amused
I have to laugh from crying
Trees mountains are arms
I am loved all day
Children grass are tears
I cry
I am loved all day
Everything
Pompous makes me laugh
I am amused often enough
In this
My beautiful green world

O there's love all day

Kenneth Patchen

NAMES OF HORSES

All winter your brute shoulders strained against collars, padding
and steerhide over the ash hames, to haul
sledges of cordwood for drying through spring and summer,
for the Glenwood stove next winter, and for the simmering
                                                        range.

In April you pulled cartloads of manure to spread on the fields,
dark manure of Holsteins, and knobs of your own clustered with
                                                        oats.
All summer you mowed the grass in meadow and hayfield, the
                                        mowing machine
clacketing beside you, while the sun walked high in the
                                        morning,

and afternoon's heat, you pulled a clawed rake through the same
                                                        acres,
gathering stacks, and dragged the wagon from stack to stack,
and the built hayrack back, up the hill to the chaffy barn,
three loads of hay a day, from standing grass in the morning.

Sundays you trotted the two miles to church, with the light load
of a quarter top buggy, and grazed in the sound of hymns.
Generation on generation, your neck rubbed the windowsill
of the stall, smoothing the wood as the sea smooths glass.

When you were old and lame, when your shoulders hurt
                                        bending to graze,
one October the man who fed you and kept you, and harnessed
                                        you every morning,
led you through corn stubble to sandy ground above Eagle Pond
and dug a hole beside you where you stood shuddering in your
                                                        skin,

and lay the shotgun's muzzle in the boneless hollow behind your
                                                              ear,
and fired the slug into your brain, and felled you into your
                                                        grave,
shoveling sand to cover you, setting goldenrod upright above
                                                          you,
where by next summer a dent in the ground made your
                                              monument.

For a hundred and fifty years, in the pasture of dead horses,
roots of pine trees pushed through the pale curves of your ribs,
yellow blossoms flourished above you in autumn, and in winter
frost heaved your bones in the ground—old toilers, soil makers:

O Roger, Mackerel, Riley, Ned, Nellie, Chester, Lady Ghost.

                                                  Donald Hall

POEM IN WHICH MY LEGS ARE ACCEPTED

Legs!
How we have suffered each other,
never meeting the standards of magazines
                            or official measurements.

I have hung you from trapezes,
     sat you on wooden rollers,
     pulled and pushed you
                            with the anxiety of taffy,
and still, you are yourselves!

Most obvious imperfection, blight on my fantasy life,
strong,
plump,
never to be skinny
or even hinting of the svelte beauties in history books
                            or Sears catalogues.
Here you are—solid, fleshy and
white as when I first noticed you, sitting on the
                  toilet, spread softly over the wooden seat,
having been with me only twelve years,
                            yet
as obvious as the legs of my thirty-year-old gym
     teacher.

Legs!
O that was the year we did acrobatics in the annual
     gym show.
How you split for me!
                  One-handed cartwheels
                  from this end of the gymnasium to
                       the other,
                  ending in double splits,

legs you flashed in blue rayon slacks my mother
  bought for the occasion
and tho you were confidently swinging along,
the rest of me blushed at the sound of clapping.

Legs!
How I have worried about you, not able to hide you,
embarrassed at beaches, in highschool
                    when the cheerleaders' slim brown legs
                                    spread all over
                                    the sand
                                    with the perfection
                                    of bamboo.
I hated you, and still you have never given out on me.
With you
I have risen to the top of blue waves,
with you
I have carried food home as a loving gift
                              when my arms began un-
                              jelling like madrilenne.

Legs, you are a pillow,
white and plentiful with feathers for his wild head.
You are the endless scenery
behind the tense sinewy elegance of his two dark legs.
You welcome him joyfully
and dance.
And you will be the locks in a new canal between
  continents.
                    The ship of life will push out of you
                    and rejoice
                        in the whiteness,
                        in the first floating and rising of water.

                                        Kathleen Fraser

I'D WANT HER EYES TO FILL WITH WONDER

I'd want her eyes to fill with wonder
I'd want her lips to open just a little
I'd want her breasts to lift at my touch

And O I'd tell her that I loved her
I'd say that the world began and ended where she was
O I'd swear that the Beautiful wept to see her naked loveliness
I'd want her thighs to put birds in my fingers
I'd want her belly to be as soft and warm as a sleeping Kitten's
I'd want her sex to meet mine as flames kissing in a dream forest

And O I'd tell her that I loved her
I'd say that all the noblest things of earth and heaven
Were made more noble because she lived
And O I'd know that the prettiest angels knelt there
As she lay asleep in my arms

Kenneth Patchen

LOVE COMES QUIETLY

Love comes quietly,
finally, drops
about me, on me,
in the old ways.

What did I know
thinking myself
able to go
alone all the way.

Robert Creeley

SLEEPING WITH SOMEONE WHO CAME IN SECRET:
(from *Eleven Tanka*)

Speak of this to no one,
not even in dreams—
and in case the pillow
should be too wise,
we'll have no pillow but our arms

Lady Ise

Translated from the Japanese
by Burton Watson

When we are like
two drunken suns
in the silence of figs
when moist night settles over
dead distant towns
when we hear the thick cry
of seeds buried
beneath layers of earth
we will build a great fire of mint
to announce the marriage
of the river's dark soul
with our endless thirst

Yvonne Caroutch

Translated from the French
by Carl Hermey

AT MID-OCEAN

All day I loved you in a fever, holding on to the tail of the
horse.
I overflowed whenever I reached out to touch you.
My hand moved over your body
covered with its dress,
burning, rough, the hand of an animal's foot moving over leaves,
the rainstorm retiring, sunlight
sliding over ocean water a thousand miles from land.

Robert Bly

from THE PRINCESS

    Now sleeps the crimson petal, now the white;
Nor waves the cypress in the palace walk;
Nor winks the gold fin in the porphyry font;
The fire-fly wakens: waken thou with me.

    Now droops the milkwhite peacock like a ghost,
And like a ghost he glimmers on to me.

    Now lies the earth all Danaë to the stars,
And all thy heart lies open unto me.

    Now slides the silent meteor on, and leaves
A shining furrow, as thy thoughts in me.

    Now folds the lily all her sweetness up,
And slips into the bosom of the lake:
So fold thyself, my dearest, thou, and slip
Into my bosom and be lost in me.

Alfred, Lord Tennyson

from RAZÓN DE AMOR

Now I love you
as the sea loves its water:
endlessly, making with it,
from outside, from
above, storms, breaks,
hollows, rests, calms.
What frenzies, loving you!
What excitement of high waves
faintings of foam going
and coming! A throng
of forms, made, unmade,
galloping dishevelled.
But behind its sides
a dream is dreaming itself,
a more profound loving
which exists below:
of not being motion now,
of ending this swaying,
this going and coming, from skies
to depths, of finding at last
the immobile flower without fall,
flower of a loving quiet, quiet.
Beyond wave and foam
the love looks for its end.
That deep place where the sea
made peace with its water;
and they're loving now
without sign, without movement.
Love
so interred in its being,

so surrendered, so still,
that our loving during life
feels sure of not ending
when kisses, gazes,
gestures cease.
As certain of not dying
as is
the immense love of the dead.

Pedro Salinas

*Translated from the Spanish
by Linda Gutierrez and
Lawrence Pitkethly*

I AM HE THAT ACHES WITH LOVE

I am he that aches with amorous love;
Does the earth gravitate?   does not all matter, aching, attract
all matter?
So the body of me to all I meet or know.

Walt Whitman

from THE SONG OF SOLOMON, Chapter 2

I am the rose of Sharon, and the lily of the valleys.

As the lily among thorns, so is my love among the daughters.

As the apple tree among the trees of the wood, so is my beloved among the sons. I sat down under his shadow with great delight, and his fruit was sweet to my taste.

He brought me to the banqueting house, and his banner over me was love.

Stay me with flagons, comfort me with apples: for I am sick of love.

His left hand is under my head, and his right hand doth embrace me.

I charge ye, O ye daughters of Jerusalem, by the roes, and by the hinds of the field, that ye stir not up, nor awake my love, till he please.

The voice of my beloved! behold, he cometh leaping upon the mountains, skipping upon the hills.

My beloved is like a roe or a young hart: behold, he standeth behind our wall, he looketh forth at the windows, shewing himself through the lattice.

My beloved spake, and said unto me, Rise up, my love, my fair one, and come away.

For lo, the winter is past, the rain is over and gone;

The flowers appear on the earth; the time of the singing of birds is come, and the voice of the turtle is heard in our land;

The fig tree putteth forth her green figs, and the vines with the tender grape give a good smell. Arise my love, my fair one, and come away.

O my dove, that art in the clefts of the rock, in the secret places of the stairs, let me see thy countenance, let me hear thy voice; for sweet is thy voice, and thy countenance is comely.

Take us the foxes, the little foxes, that spoil the vines: for our vines have tender grapes.

My beloved is mine, and I am his: he feedeth among the lilies.

Until the day break, and the shadows flee away, turn, my beloved, and be thou like a roe or a young hart upon the mountains of Bether.

HE REMEMBERS FORGOTTEN BEAUTY

When my arms wrap you round I press
My heart upon the loveliness
That has long faded from the world;
The jewelled crowns that kings have hurled
In shadowy pools, when armies fled;
The love-tales wrought with silken thread
By dreaming ladies upon cloth
That has made fat the murderous moth;
The roses that of old time were
Woven by ladies in their hair,
The dew-cold lilies ladies bore
Through many a sacred corridor
Where such grey clouds of incense rose
That only God's eyes did not close:
For that pale breast and lingering hand
Come from a more dream-heavy land,
A more dream-heavy hour than this;
And when you sigh from kiss to kiss
I hear white Beauty sighing, too,
For hours when all must fade like dew,
But flame on flame, and deep on deep,
Throne over throne where in half sleep,
Their swords upon their iron knees,
Brood her high lonely mysteries.

William Butler Yeats

THE DREAM

I

I met her as a blossom on a stem
Before she ever breathed, and in that dream
The mind remembers from a deeper sleep:
Eye learned from eye, cold lip from sensual lip.
My dream divided on a point of fire;
Light hardened on the water where we were;
A bird sang low; the moonlight sifted in;
The water rippled, and she rippled on.

II

She came toward me in the flowing air,
A shape of change, encircled by its fire.
I watched her there, between me and the moon;
The bushes and the stones danced on and on;
I touched her shadow when the light delayed;
I turned my face away, and yet she stayed.
A bird sang from the center of a tree;
She loved the wind because the wind loved me.

III

Love is not love until love's vulnerable.
She slowed to sigh, in that long interval.
A small bird flew in circles where we stood;
The deer came down, out of the dappled wood.
All who remember, doubt. Who calls that strange?
I tossed a stone, and listened to its plunge.
She knew the grammar of least motion, she
Lent me one virtue, and I live thereby.

IV

She held her body steady in the wind;
Our shadows met, and slowly swung around;
She turned the field into a glittering sea;
I played in flame and water like a boy
And I swayed out beyond the white seafoam;
Like a wet log, I sang within a flame.
In that last while, eternity's confine,
I came to love, I came into my own.

Theodore Roethke

LULLABY

Lay your sleeping head, my love,
Human on my faithless arm;
Time and fevers burn away
Individual beauty from
Thoughtful children, and the grave
Proves the child ephemeral:
But in my arms till break of day
Let the living creature lie,
Mortal, guilty, but to me
The entirely beautiful.

Soul and body have no bounds:
To lovers as they lie upon
Her tolerant enchanted slope
In their ordinary swoon,
Grave the vision Venus sends
Of supernatural sympathy,
Universal love and hope;
While an abstract insight wakes
Among the glaciers and the rocks
The hermit's sensual ecstasy.

Certainty, fidelity
On the stroke of midnight pass
Like vibrations of a bell,
And fashionable madmen raise
Their pedantic boring cry:
Every farthing of the cost,
All the dreaded cards foretell,
Shall be paid, but from this night
Not a whisper, not a thought,
Not a kiss nor look be lost.

Beauty, midnight, vision dies:
Let the winds of dawn that blow
Softly round your dreaming head
Such a day of sweetness show
Eye and knocking heart may bless,
Find the mortal world enough:
Noons of dryness see you fed
By the involuntary powers,
Nights of insult let you pass
Watched by every human love.

W. H. Auden

POEM

to Franz Kline

I will always love you
though I never loved you

a boy smelling faintly of heather
staring up at your window

the passion that enlightens
and stills and cultivates, gone

while I sought your face
to be familiar in the blueness

or to follow your sharp whistle
around a corner into my light

that was love growing fainter
each time you failed to appear

I spent my whole self searching
love which I thought was you
it was mine so briefly
and I never knew it, or you went

I thought it was outside disappearing
but it is disappearing in my heart

like snow blown in a window
to be gone from the world

I will always love you

Frank O'Hara

SONG

Reading about the Wisconsin Weeping Willow
I was thinking of you
and when I saw Plus Free Gifts
I was thinking of you
and when farther down the page I saw Eat Five Kinds of
                                Apples from Just One Miracle Tree
I was thinking of you
I was thinking of you

Ruth Krauss

INANNA'S SONG

He has sprouted; he has burgeoned;
He is lettuce planted by the water.
He is the one my flesh loves best.
My well-stocked garden of the plain;
My barley growing high in its furrow.
My apple tree which bears fruit up to its crown;
He is lettuce planted by the water.

My honey-man, my honey-man sweetens me always.
My lord, the honey-man of the gods;
He is the one my flesh loves best.
His hand is honey, his foot is honey;
He sweetens me always.

My eager impetuous caresser of the navel,
My caresser of the soft thighs,
He sweetens me always,
He is lettuce planted by the water.

*Translated from the ancient Sumerian (2000 B.C.)
by Diane Wolkstein and Samuel Noah Kramer*

SONG

Sweet beast, I have gone prowling,
 a proud rejected man
who lived along the edges
 catch as catch can;
in darkness and in hedges
 I sang my sour tone
and all my love was howling
 conspicuously alone.

I curled and slept all day
 or nursed my bloodless wounds
until the squares were silent
 where I could make my tunes
singular and violent.
 Then, sure as hearers came
I crept and flinched away.
 And, girl, you've done the same.

A stray from my own type,
 led along by blindness,
my love was near to spoiled
 and curdled all my kindness.
I find no kin, no child;
 only the weasel's ilk.
Sweet beast, cat of my own stripe,
 come and take my milk.

     W. D. Snodgrass

SIMPLE-SONG

When we are going toward someone we say
you are just like me
your thoughts are my brothers
word matches word
how easy to be together.

When we are leaving someone we say
how strange you are
we cannot communicate
we can never agree
how hard, hard and weary to be together.

We are not different nor alike
but each strange in his leather body
sealed in skin and reaching out clumsy hands
and loving is an act
that cannot outlive
the open hand
the open eye
the door in the chest standing open.

Marge Piercy

THE HARDNESS SCALE

Diamonds are forever so I gave you quartz
which is #7 on the hardness scale
and it's hard enough to get to know anybody these days
if only to scratch the surface
and quartz will scratch six other mineral surfaces:
it will scratch glass
it will scratch gold
it will even
scratch your eyes out one morning—you can't be
too careful.
Diamonds are industrial so I bought
a ring of topaz
which is #8 on the hardness scale.
I wear it on my right hand, the way it was
supposed to be, right?   No tears and fewer regrets
for reasons smooth and clear as glass.   Topaz will
                    scratch glass,
it will scratch your quartz,
and all your radio crystals.   You'll have to be silent
the rest of your days
not to mention your nights.   Not to mention
the night you ran away very drunk very
very drunk and you tried to cross the border
but couldn't make it across the lake.
Stirring up geysers with the oars you drove the red canoe
in circles, tried to pole it but
your left hand didn't know
what the right hand was doing.
You fell asleep
and let everyone know it when you woke up.
In a gin-soaked morning (hair of the dog) you went
hunting for geese,
shot three lake trout in violation of the game laws,

told me to clean them and that
my eyes were bright as sapphires
which is #9 on the hardness scale.
A sapphire will cut a pearl
it will cut stainless steel
it will cut vinyl and mylar and will probably
cut a record this fall
to be released on an obscure label known only to aficionados.
I will buy a copy.
I may buy you a copy
depending on how your tastes have changed.
I will buy copies for my friends
we'll get a new needle,
a diamond needle,
which is #10 on the hardness scale
and will cut anything.
It will cut wood and mortar,
plaster and iron,
it will cut the sapphires in my eyes and I will bleed
blind as 4 A.M. in the subways when even degenerates
are dreaming, blind as the time
you shot up the room with a new hunting rifle
blind drunk
as you were.
You were #11 on the hardness scale
later that night
apologetic as
you worked your way up
slowly from the knees
and you worked your way down
from the open-throated blouse.
Diamonds are forever so I give you softer things.

Joyce Peseroff

PERVERSITY

Oh I want to
tell you
how you have
hurt me,
to describe every
point of exquisite
pain and to
what end?
So you will
take me in
your arms and
then
let me
stroke your sweet hair.

Susan Griffin

SONG

Dew on the bamboos,
Cooler than dew on the bamboos
Is putting my cheek against your breasts.

The pit of green and black snakes,
I would rather be in the pit of green and black snakes
Than be in love with you.

Translated from the 5th-century Sanskrit by Edward Powys Mathers

BETROTHED

You have put your two hands upon me, and your mouth,
You have said my name as a prayer.
Here where trees are planted by the water
I have watched your eyes, cleansed from regret,
And your lips, closed over all that love cannot say.

My mother remembers the agony of her womb
And long years that seemed to promise more than
this.
She says, "You do not love me,
You do not want me,
You will go away."

In the country whereto I go
I shall not see the face of my friend
Nor her hair the color of sunburnt grasses;
Together we shall not find
The land on whose hills bends the new moon
In air traversed of birds.

What have I thought of love?
I have said, "It is beauty and sorrow."
I have thought that it would bring me lost delights, and
splendor
As a wind out of old time. . . .

But there is only the evening here,
And the sound of willows
Now and again dipping their long oval leaves in the water.

Louise Bogan

PEOPLE

Not all the time
But when I realize
You don't love me,
I want to see you
From my mother's lap
The way I watched people
When I was small.

Orhan Veli Kanik
Translated from the Turkish
by Talat Sait Halman

Western Wind, when wilt thou blow,
The small rain down can rain?
Christ, if my love were in my arms
And I in my bed again!

Anonymous, Early English

ON LOVE: (from *Twenty-Three Tanka*)

So great the pain,
I've passed the days
without speaking of sorrow,
till my thoughts are worn out
and I no longer hate you

Kyōgoku Tamekane

Translated from the Japanese
by Burton Watson

MIRAGE

The hope I dreamed of was a dream,
    Was but a dream; and now I wake,
Exceeding comfortless, and worn, and old,
    For a dream's sake.

I hang my harp upon a tree,
    A weeping willow in a lake;
I hang my silenced harp there, wrung and snapt
    For a dream's sake.

Lie still, lie still, my breaking heart;
    My silent heart, lie still and break:
Life, and the world, and mine own self, are changed
    For a dream's sake.

Christina Rossetti

BEING SAD

I might have resented
The people I love
If love
Hadn't taught me
To be sad and to stay sad.

Orhan Veli Kanik

*Translated from the Turkish
by Talat Sait Halman*

from THE WALLS DO NOT FALL

O heart, small urn
of porphyry, agate or cornelian,

how imperceptibly the grain fell
between a heart-beat of pleasure

and a heart-beat of pain;
I do not know how it came

nor how long it had lain there,
nor can I say

how it escaped tempest
of passion and malice,

nor why it was not washed away
in flood of sorrow,

or dried up in the bleak drought
of bitter thought.

H.D.

LOCK THE PLACE IN YOUR HEART

Lock the place in your heart
into which I have poured my emotions

I do not want to be hurt again
use your heartbeat as the key
only you can hear if it unlocks itself

If the wind around you
should blow away
breathe into it and let my secrets go

Zindzi Mandela
South Africa

HEART! WE WILL FORGET HIM

Heart! We will forget him!
You and I—tonight!
You may forget the warmth he gave—
I will forget the light!

When you have done, pray tell me
That I may straight begin!
Haste! lest while you're lagging
I remember him!

Emily Dickinson

A heart that's been broken
has a tiny hinge
And when it happens a
second or third time
it just
swings open & shut
like a gate.

Maureen Owen

THE ALCHEMIST

I burned my life, that I might find
A passion wholly of the mind,
Thought divorced from eye and bone,
Ecstasy come to breath alone.
I broke my life, to seek relief
From the flawed light of love and grief.

With mounting beat the utter fire
Charred existence and desire.
It died low, ceased its sudden thresh.
I had found unmysterious flesh—
Not the mind's avid substance—still
Passionate beyond the will.

Louise Bogan

THE WINTER MOON

I hit my wife and went out and saw
the moon like ten thousand lanterns.

Over the soft snow after a snowstorm
I am walking without any idea where I am going.

   —What is it makes me hate so hard?
     When we hate, we are more serious than
        when we love.
     So now why am I starting to feel I
        love her again?

Everything is like that snowstorm.
When it is over, we see
The moon like a thousand lanterns.

Tagaki Kyozo

Translated from the Japanese by James Kirkup
and Nakamo Michio

from 9 VERSES OF THE SAME SONG

and my love has come to me
to ask for my comfort
for the hurt I give her
—having no other

time and again

for that trammel me
my heart

my hearing suffers
no more sorrowing music

Wendell Berry

SWAHILI LOVE SONG

If only
The heart had a lid
I would have opened it
and shown you my grief,
and you would have known
if I am
the one for you.

Anonymous

Translated from the Swahili
by Jan Knappert

INSOMNIA

The moon in the bureau mirror
looks out a million miles
(and perhaps with pride, at herself,
but she never, never smiles)
far and away beyond sleep, or
perhaps she's a daytime sleeper.

By the Universe deserted,
she'd tell it to go to hell,
and she'd find a body of water,
or a mirror, on which to dwell.
So wrap up care in a cobweb
and drop it down the well.

into that world inverted
where left is always right,
where the shadows are really the body,
where we stay awake all night,
where the heavens are shallow as the sea
is now deep, and you love me.

Elizabeth Bishop

GIRL'S SONG

O my cousin, my beloved,

Once I thought I did not love you.
When they came back saying they had left you dead,
I went up on the hill where my tomb will be.
I gathered stones, I buried my heart.
The odor of you that I smell between my breasts
Shoots fire into my bones.

Tuareg, from the Sahara
Translated from the Taitok by Willard Trask

END SONG

When you break your heart it changes
all exits are open arriving like a sky
each evening light goes down more beautiful
than the one that was
the world changes when it comes to an end
a dream bends when the night in it dissolves

When first I saw my world I threw my arms around it

When you break your heart it changes
all exits are open arriving like a sky
each evening light goes down more beautiful
than the one that was the world
changes when it comes to an end a dream
bends when the night in it dissolves

Ruth Krauss

"Don't touch me!" I scream at passers-by—
they do not even notice me.
Cursing the rooms of other people,
I hang about their anterooms.

But who will knock a window through?
Who will hold out his hand to me?
I am roasting over a slow fire.

Natalya Gorbanyevskaya
Translated from the Russian by Daniel Weissbort

A PAINFUL LOVE SONG

While we were together
we were like a pair of scissors,
good and very useful.

After we separated
we became again
two sharp knives
stuck deeply into the world's flesh,
each one at his place.

Yehuda Amichai

Translated from the Hebrew
by the poet

What lips my lips have kissed, and where, and why,
I have forgotten, and what arms have lain
Under my head till morning; but the rain
Is full of ghosts tonight, that tap and sigh
Upon the glass and listen for reply,
And in my heart there stirs a quiet pain
For unremembered lads that not again
Will turn to me at midnight with a cry.
Thus in the winter stands the lonely tree,
Nor knows what birds have vanished one by one,
Yet knows its boughs more silent than before:
I cannot say what loves have come and gone;
I only know that summer sang in me
A little while, that in me sings no more.

Edna St. Vincent Millay

EPILOGUE

I thought I had found a swan
but it was a migrating snow-goose.

I thought I was linked invisibly to another's life
but I found myself more alone with him than without him.

I thought I had found a fire
but it was the play of light on bright stones.

I thought I was wounded to the core
but I was only bruised.

Denise Levertov

SEIZURE

To me that man equals a god
as he sits before you and listens
closely to your sweet voice

and lovely laughter—which troubles
the heart in my ribs. For now
as I look at you my voice fails,

my tongue is broken and thin fire
runs like a thief through my body.
My eyes are dead to light, my ears

pound, and sweat pours down over me.
I shudder, I am paler than grass,
and am intimate with dying—but

I must suffer everything, being poor.

Sappho

Translated from the Greek
by Willis Barnstone

COLORS

When your face
appeared over my crumpled life
at first I understood
only the poverty of what I have.
Then its particular light
on woods, on rivers, on the sea,
became my beginning in the colored world
in which I had not yet had my beginning.
I am so frightened, I am so frightened,
of the unexpected sunrise finishing,
of revelations
and tears and the excitement finishing.
I don't fight it, my love is this fear
I nourish it who can nourish nothing,
love's slipshod watchman.
Fear hems me in.
I am conscious that these minutes are short
and that the colors in my eyes will vanish
when your face sets.

Yevgeny Yevtushenko

Translated from the Russian
by Robin Milner-Gulland and Peter Levi, S.J.

Love wears roses' elegance,
The lilies move themselves to dance,
Their beauty lies within them.
They take their place, and dance with grace,
When love comes in between them.

Who understands the exalted dance,
The bowing, bending waiting stance,
The spinning round forever?
The mincing pace, the whirling space,
The flight that ceases never?

For love may stop, and love may hop,
And love may sing, and love may spring,
And love may rest in loving,
And love may sleep, and love may leap;
What mind can follow, proving?

Sister Bertke, Hermitess of Utrecht

GHAZAL XII

I am not a flower of song
      nor any of the bright shuttles of music
I am the sound of my own breaking

You think of how your hair looks
I think of the end of things

We think we know our own minds
but our hearts are children

Now that you have appeared to me I bow
may you be blessed

You look after the wretched
no wonder you came
      looking for me

Mirza Ghalib

*Translated from the Urdu
by W. S. Merwin with Aijaz Ahmad*

THE FIST

The fist clenched round my heart
loosens a little, and I gasp
brightness; but it tightens
again. When have I ever not loved
the pain of love? But this has moved

past love to mania. This has the strong
clench of the madman, this is
gripping the ledge of unreason, before
plunging howling into the abyss.

Hold hard then, heart. This way at least you live.

Derek Walcott

TO CARRY ON LIVING

Oh, make my bed in the warm air,
let my head rest in heaven
which once was ancient water.

Think about this world
which has done its best
to calm us
so we won't suffer too much
in years to come.

To carry on living is
to avoid meeting
each other again.

Yehuda Amichai
Translated from the Hebrew by the poet

THE RADIANCE

I talk to my inner lover, and I say, why such rush?
We sense that there is some sort of spirit
that loves birds and animals and the ants.
Perhaps the same one who gave a radiance to you in your
                                               mother's womb.
Is it logical you would be walking around entirely orphaned
                                                      now?

The truth is you turned away yourself,
And decided to go into the dark alone.
Now you are tangled up in others, and have forgotten what
                                              you once knew,
and that's why everything you do has some weird failure in it.

Kabir

Translated from the Hindi by Robert Bly

MOVEMENT

Towards not being
anyone else's center
of gravity.
        A wanting
to love: not
to lean over towards
an other, and fall,
but feel within one
a flexible steel
upright, parallel
to the spine but
longer, from which to stretch;
one's own
grave springboard; the outflying spirit's
vertical trampoline.

Denise Levertov

A BLESSING

Just off the highway to Rochester, Minnesota,
Twilight bounds softly forth on the grass.
And the eyes of those two Indian ponies
Darken with kindness.
They have come gladly out of the willows
To welcome my friend and me.
We step over the barbed wire into the pasture
Where they have been grazing all day, alone.
They ripple tensely, then can hardly contain their happiness
That we have come.
They bow shyly as wet swans. They love each other.
There is no loneliness like theirs.
At home once more,
They begin munching the young tufts of spring in the darkness.
I would like to hold the slenderer one in my arms,
For she has walked over to me
And nuzzled my left hand.
She is black and white,
Her mane falls wild on her forehead,
And the light breeze moves me to caress her long ear
That is delicate as the skin over a girl's wrist.
Suddenly I realize
That if I stepped out of my body I would break
Into blossom.

James Wright

Love you alone have been with us
        since before the beginning of the world

tell us all the secrets one by one
        we are of the same Household as you

In dread of your fire we closed our mouths
        and gave up words

but you are not fire
        you are without flames

Moment by moment
        you destroy the city of the mind

gust of wind to the mind's candle
        wine for the fire-worshippers

Friend with friends
        enemy with enemies

or somewhere between the two
        looking for both

To the sane
        the words of lovers are nothing but stories

if that was all you were
        how could you turn night into day

You whose beauty sends the world reeling
        your love brings about all this confusion

You are that love's masterpiece
        you make it clear

Oh sun of God
        sultan of sultans
        glory and joy of Tabriz

you give light to those on earth
        beauty and splendor of the age

Rumi

Translated from the Persian
by W. S. Merwin with Talat Sait Halman

The whole universe is full of God
    yet His truth is seen by no one
    you have to look for Him in yourself
    you and he are not separate you are one

The other world is what can't be seen
    here on earth we must live as well as we can
    exile is grieving and anguish
    no one comes back who has once gone

Come let us be friends this one time
    let life be our friend
    let us be lovers of each other
    the earth will be left to no one

You know what Yunus is saying
    its meaning is in the ear of your heart
    we should all live truly here
    for we will not live here forever

Yunus Emre

Translated from the Turkish
by W. S. Merwin and Talat Sait Halman

THINGS I DIDN'T KNOW I LOVED

it's 1962 March 28th
I'm sitting by the window on the Prague-Berlin train
night is falling
I never knew I liked
night descending like a tired bird on the smoky wet plain
I don't like
likening the descent of evening to that of a tired bird

I didn't know I loved the soil
can someone who hasn't worked the soil love it
I've never worked the soil
it must be my only Platonic love

and here I've loved the river all this time
whether motionless like this it curls skirting the hills
European hills topped off with chateaus
or whether it stretches out flat as far as the eye can see
I know you can't wash in the same river even once
I know the river will bring new lights that you will not see
I know we live slightly longer than a horse and not nearly
                                            as long as a crow
I know this has troubled people before
                              and will trouble those after me
I know all this has been said a thousand times before
                              and will be said after me

I didn't know I liked the sky
cloudy or clear
the blue vault that Andrei watched on his back on the
                              battlefield at Borodino
in prison I translated both volumes of *War and Peace* into
                              Turkish
I hear voices
not from the blue vault but from the yard
the guards are beating someone again

I didn't know I loved trees
bare beeches around Moscow in Peredelkino
they come upon me in winter noble and modest
beeches are counted as Russian the way we count poplars as
                                                    Turkish

"the poplars of Izmir
losing their leaves . . .
they call us The Knife—
                    lover like a young tree . . .
we blow stately mansions sky-high"
Ilgaz forest, 1920: I tied a linen handkerchief edged with
                                        embroidery to a pine bough

I never knew I loved roads
even the asphalt kind
Vera's behind the wheel we're driving from Moscow to the
                                                    Crimea
                                        Koktebele
                    formerly "Göktepe ili" in Turkish
the two of us inside a closed box
the world flows past on both sides distant and mute
I was never this close to anyone in my life
bandits came upon me on the red road between Bolu and
                                        Gerede and I am eighteen
apart from my life I don't have anything in the wagon that
                                                    they can take
and at eighteen our lives are what we value least
I've written this somewhere before
wading through the dark muddy street I'm going to the
                                                    Karagöz

Ramazan night
the paper lantern leading the way
maybe nothing like this ever happened
maybe I read it somewhere an eight-year-old boy going to the
                                                    shadow play

Ramazan night in Istanbul holding his grandfather's hand
       his grandfather has on a fez and is wearing the fur coat
          with the sable collar over his robe
       and there's a lantern in the servant's hand
     and I can't contain myself for joy
flowers come to mind for some reason
poppies cactuses jonquils
in the jonquil garden in Kadiköy Istanbul I kissed Marika
fresh almonds on her breath
I'm seventeen
my heart on a swing touched the sky
I didn't know I loved flowers
friends sent me three red carnations in prison
I just remembered the stars
I love them too
whether I'm floored watching them from below
or whether I'm flying by their side

I have some questions for the cosmonauts
did they see the stars much larger
were they like huge jewels on black velvet
                    or apricots on orange
does it make a person feel proud to get a little closer
                                        to the stars
I saw color photos of the cosmos in Ogonek magazine
now don't get upset friends but nonfigurative shall we say or
abstract well some of them looked just like such paintings
which is to say they were terribly figurative and concrete
my heart was in my mouth looking at them
they are the endlessness of our longing to grasp things
looking at them I could think even of death and not feel one
                                        bit sad
I never knew I loved the cosmos

snow flashes in front of my eyes
both heavy wet steady snow and the dry whirling kind
I didn't know I liked snow
I never knew I loved the sun
even when setting cherry-red as now
in Istanbul too it sometimes sets in postcard colors
but you aren't about to paint it like that

I didn't know I loved the sea
                                    or how much
—putting aside the Sea of Azov

I didn't know I loved the clouds
whether I'm under or up above them
whether they look like giants or shaggy white beasts

moonlight the most false the most languid the most petit-
                                    bourgeois
strikes me
I like it
I didn't know I liked rain
whether it falls like a fine net or splatters against the glass
my heart leaves me tangled up in a net or trapped inside a drop
and takes off for uncharted countries I didn't know I loved
rain but why did I suddenly discover all these passions sitting
by the window on the Prague-Berlin train
is it because I lit my sixth cigarette
one alone is enough to kill me
is it because I'm almost dead from thinking about someone
                                    back in Moscow
her hair straw-blond eyelashes blue

the train plunges on through the pitch-black night
I never knew I liked the night pitch-black
sparks fly from the engine
I didn't know I loved sparks
I didn't know I loved so many things and I had to wait until I
was sixty to find it out sitting by the window on the Prague-
Berlin train watching the world disappear as if on a journey
from which one does not return

19 April 1962 Moscow

Nazim Hikmet
Translated from the Turkish
by Randy Blasing and Mutlu Konuk

Amichai, Yehuda, *56, 64*
Anonymous (Ancient Sumerian), *35*
Anonymous (Azande), *3*
Anonymous (Early English), *43*
Anonymous (Old Testament), *28*
Anonymous (Sanskrit), *41*
Anonymous (Swahili), *52*
Anonymous (Tuareg), *54*
Arbiter, Petronius, *7*
Auden, W. H., *32*

Berry, Wendell, *51*
Bertke, Sister, *61*
Bhavabhūti, *15*
Bishop, Elizabeth, *53*
Bly, Robert, *24*
Bogan, Louise, *42, 49*

Caroutch, Yvonne, *24*
Creeley, Robert, *23*
Cummings, E. E., *14, 16*

D., H., *10, 46*
Dickinson, Emily, *47*

Emre, Yunus, *70*

Fraser, Kathleen, *20*

Ghalib, Mirza, *62*
Gorbanyevskaya, Natalya, *55*
Griffin, Susan, *12, 40*

Hall, Donald, *13, 18*
Hikmet, Nazim, *71*
Hughes, Ted, *2, 6*

Ise, Lady, *23*
Izumi, Lady, *5*

Kabir, *65*
Kanik, Orhan Veli, *43, 45*
Krauss, Ruth, *35, 55*
Kyozo, Tagaki, *50*

Levertov, Denise, *58, 66*

Mandela, Zindzi, *47*
Millay, Edna St. Vincent, *57*
Morgan, Edwin, *1*

O'Hara, Frank, *34*
Otomo, Lady, *12*
Owen, Maureen, *48*

Patchen, Kenneth, *17, 22*
Peseroff, Joyce, *38*
Piercy, Marge, *37*

Radnoti, Miklos, *4, 8, 11*
Roethke, Theodore, *30*
Rossetti, Christina, *45*
Rumi, *68*

Sabines, Jaime, *3*
Salinas, Pedro, *26*
Sappho, *59*
Snodgrass, W. D., *36*

Tamekane, Kyoguku, *44*
Tennyson, Alfred, Lord, *25*

Walcott, Derek, *63*
Whitman, Walt, *27*
Wright, James, *67*

Yeats, William Butler, *9, 29*
Yen, Hsiao, *9*
Yevtushenko, Yevgeny, *5, 60*

Alchemist, The, *49*
At Mid-Ocean, *24*

Being Sad, *45*
Betrothed, *42*
Blessing, A, *67*
Brown Penny, *9*

Charm, *4*
Colors, *60*

Dream, The, *30*

End Song, *55*
Epilogue, *58*

Fist, The, *63*

Ghazal XII, *62*
Girl's Song, *54*

Hardness Scale, The, *38*
Heart! We Will Forget Him, *47*
He Remembers Forgotten
  Beauty, *29*
Hesitating Ode, *8*
His Legs Ran About, *6*

I Am He That Aches With
  Love, *27*
I'd Want Her Eyes to Fill With
  Wonder, *22*
I Hid You, *11*
Inanna's Song, *35*
Insomnia, *53*

Lock the Place in Your Heart,
  47
Love, *5*
Love Comes Quietly, *23*
Lullaby, *32*

Mirage, *45*
Movement, *66*

Names of Horses, *18*
9 Verses of the Same Song,
  from, *51*
#15 from Nineteen Pieces for
  Love, *12*

On Love, *44*

Painful Love Song, A, *56*
People, *43*
Perversity, *40*
Poem, *34*
Poem in Which My Legs Are
  Accepted, *20*
Princess, The, from, *25*

Radiance, The, *65*
Razón de Amor, from, *26*

Seizure, *59*
Simple-Song, *37*
Sleeping With Someone Who
  Came in Secret, *23*
Song (Azande), *3*
Song (Ted Hughes), *2*
Song (Ruth Krauss), *35*
Song (Sanskrit), *41*
Song (W. D. Snodgrass), *36*
Song of Solomon, The, from,
  28
Spring Song of Tzu-yeh, A, *9*
Strawberries, *1*
Swahili Love Song, *52*

Things I Didn't Know I Loved,
  71
To Carry On Living, *64*

Unknown Love, *12*
Untitled (Anonymous, Early
   English), *43*
Untitled (Petronius Arbiter), *7*
Untitled (Sister Bertke), *61*
Untitled (Bhavabhūti), *15*
Untitled (Yvonne Caroutch), *24*
Untitled (E. E. Cummings), *14*
Untitled (E. E. Cummings), *16*
Untitled (Yunus Emre), *70*
Untitled (Natalya
   Gorbanyevskaya), *55*
Untitled (Edna St. Vincent
   Millay), *57*

Untitled (Maureen Owen), *48*
Untitled (Rumi), *68*

Valentine, *13*

Waiting, *5*
Walls Do Not Fall, The, from,
   46
What There Is, *17*
White World, *10*
Winter Moon, The, *50*

You Have What I Look For, *3*

A heart that's been broken, *48*
All day I loved you in a fever, holding on to the tail of the horse, *24*
All winter your brute shoulders strained against collars, padding, *18*
and my love has come to me, *51*

Chipmunks jump, and, *13*

Deep in love, *15*
Desire for a woman took hold of me in the night, *3*
Dew on the bamboos, *41*
Diamonds are forever so I gave you quartz, *38*
Doing, a filthy pleasure is, and short, *7*
"Don't touch me!" I scream at passersby, *55*

Heart! We will forget him!, *47*
He has sprouted; he has burgeoned;, *35*

I am he that aches with amorous love, *27*
I am not a flower of song, *62*
I am the rose of Sharon, and the lily of the valleys, *28*
I burned my life, that I might find, *49*
I'd want her eyes to fill with wonder, *22*
If I speak of love you'll think I am like everyone else, but my heart, *5*
If only, *52*
I hid you for a long time, *11*

I hit my wife and went out and saw, *50*
I like my body when it is with your, *14*
I met her as a blossom on a stem, *30*
I might have resented, *45*
In this my green world, *17*
I talk to my inner lover, and I say, why such rush, *65*
I thought I had found a swan, *58*
it's 1962 March 28th, *71*
I've been planning to tell you, *8*
I whispered, "I am too young.", *9*
I will always love you, *34*

Just off the highway to Rochester, Minnesota, *67*

Lay your sleeping head, my love, *32*
Legs!, *20*
Lock the place in your heart, *47*
Love comes quietly, *23*
Love wears roses' elegance, *61*
Love you alone have been with us, *68*

My love will come, *5*

Not all the time, *43*
Now I love you, *26*
Now sleeps the crimson petal, now the white, *25*

O heart, small urn, *46*
Oh I want to, *40*
Oh, make my bed in the warm air, *64*

O lady, when the tipped cup of
   the moon blessed you, *2*
O my cousin, my beloved, *54*
On the stairway fragrance assails
   the bosom, *9*

Reading about the Wisconsin
   Weeping Willow, *35*

So great the pain, *44*
Speak of this to no one, *23*
Sweet beast, I have gone
   prowling, *36*

The fist clenched round my
   heart, *63*
The hope I dreamed of was a
   dream, *45*
The moon in the bureau mirror,
   53
There were never strawberries, *1*
The whole universe is full of
   God, *70*
The whole white world is ours, *10*
Till they tangled and seemed to
   trip and lie down, *6*

To me that man equals a god, *59*
Towards not being, *66*
trying to say, *12*

Unknown love, *12*

Western Wind, when wilt thou
   blow, *43*
What lips my lips have kissed,
   and where, and why, *57*
When my arms wrap you round
   I press, *29*
When we are going toward
   someone we say, *37*
When we are like, *24*
When you break your heart it
   changes, *55*
When your face, *60*
While we were together, *56*
With trembling eyes, *4*

You have put your two hands
   upon me, and your mouth, *42*
You have what I look for, what
   I long for, what I love, *3*
your little voice, *16*